mrjc

W9-AMU-314

The Search
for the
Titanic
Finding the Ship's Watery Grave

by Terri Dougherty

CONTENT CONSULTANT:
Captain Charles Weeks
Professor Emeritus in Marine Transportation
Maine Maritime Academy

CAPSTONE PRESS
a capstone imprint

Velocity Books are published by Capstone Press,
1710 Roe Crest Drive, North Mankato, Minnesota 56003
www.capstonepub.com

Library of Congress Cataloging-in-Publication Data
Cataloging-in-publication information is on file with the Library of Congress.
ISBN 978-1-4914-0418-8 (library binding)
ISBN 978-1-4914-0422-5 (ebook PDF)

Editorial Credits
Lauren Coss, editor; Craig Hinton, designer; Nikki Farinella, production specialist

Photo Credits
AP Images: 21, 23 (top right), 36, 45, Mike Kullen, 10 (top), National Ocean and Atmospheric Administration, 39, Woods Hole Oceanographic Inst., 43 (bottom); Corbis: Bettmann, 15 (top), 20, 28, Ralph White, 4–5, 18–19 (top), 23 (top left), 23 (bottom), 24, 26–27, 37 (middle), 38; Getty Images: Pierre Mion/National Geographic, 12 (top); Painting © Ken Marschall, cover, 7 (top); Library of Congress: 8, 9 (bottom right), Theodor Horydczak, 7 (middle); National Geographic Creative: Emory Kristof, 19 (bottom), 31, 32, 34 (top); National Oceanic and Atmospheric Administration: 12 (bottom), 13, 16, Ed Bowlby/OAR/Office of Ocean Exploration, 17 (bottom), OAR/National Undersea Research Program/Woods Hole Oceanographic Inst., 22 (left), Quartermaster Joseph Schebal, 22 (right); Newscom: BP/UPI, 17 (top), Dennis Van Tine/ABACAUSA.com, 25, Discovery Channel/RMS Titanic Inc./AFP, 33, 37 (top), Dorling Kindersley Universal Images Group, 42, GDA/El Tiempo, 11 (top), Matthew Tulloch KRT, 40, PMG/SIPA, 44, Richard B. Levine, 41 (top right), 41 (top left), 41 (bottom right), Ron Asadorian/Splash News, 41 (bottom left), SH1 Wenn Photos, 5, Thomas Kleindinst, 34–35 (bottom); Red Line Editorial, 14, 29, 30; Shutterstock Images: Olga Popova, 6; SuperStock: Universal Images Group, 43 (top); Thinkstock: Dorling Kindersley, 8–9 (bottom), 10–11 (middle), filo 8 (ship icon), iStockphoto, 29 (map), perysty, 15 (bottom)

Artistic Effects
Shutterstock Images

Source Notes
Page 33 • Robert Ballard, from *Return to Titanic: A New Look at the World's Most Famous Lost Ship*, by Robert D. Ballard with Michael S. Sweeney. Washington, D.C.: National Geographic, 2004. Page 41.; Page 45 (top left) • Edward Kamuda, quoted in "Titanic at 100: Be Among the Last to Dive to the Wreck Site?" by Brian Handwerk, as published on *National Geographic Daily News* on April 6, 2012. http://news.nationalgeographic.com/news/2012/04/120406-titanic-100-anniversary-bob-ballard-science/; Page 45 (top right) • Rob McCallum, quoted in "Titanic at 100: Be Among the Last to Dive to the Wreck Site?" by Brian Handwerk, as published on *National Geographic Daily News* on April 6, 2012. http://news.nationalgeographic.com/news/2012/04/120406-titanic-100-anniversary-bob-ballard-science; Page 45 (bottom left) • Eva Hart, as quoted in "Eva Hart, 91, a Last Survivor with Memory of *Titanic* Dies," by Robert McG. Thomas Jr., as published in the *New York Times* on February 6, 1996. Accessed at the New York Times. http://www.nytimes.com/1996/02/16/world/eva-hart-91-a-last-survivor-with-memory-of-titanic-dies.html?ref=titanic; Page 45 (bottom right) • Robert DiSogra, quoted in "Titanic International Works to Recover Objects from Wreck," by Edward Colimore, as published in *Boca Raton News* on December 11, 1994. Page 12A.

Printed in the United States of America in Stevens Point, Wisconsin.
032014   008092WZF14

Table of Contents

Glimpsing *Titanic*

The time was shortly after midnight on September 1, 1985. Crew members aboard *Knorr* kept a close eye on video screens in the ship's control center. Murky images of the muddy ocean bottom glowed on every monitor. Everyone eagerly waited for a sign they were near *Titanic*.

For days Robert Ballard, the expedition's head scientist, and the crew had been watching for any hint they were close to the great ship. They were starting to lose hope. Would they ever find *Titanic*?

One of *Titanic*'s boilers lies on the ocean floor, approximately 370 miles (600 kilometers) off the coast of Newfoundland, Canada.

boiler—a device that creates steam to power a ship's engine

FACT: *Titanic* sank at 2:20 a.m. on April 15, 1912. It was discovered at almost the same time of day. When Ballard and his crew realized this fact, they observed a few moments of silence in honor of those who died in the disaster.

Then at 12:48 a.m., a metal object came into view. Could it have fallen from the huge ship as it sank? Hopes rose as more objects streamed past on the monitors. A few minutes after 1:00 a.m., a clear image of a boiler appeared. The crew jumped and cheered. The boiler's plate matched photos of the ones on the doomed ship.

Seventy-three years after *Titanic* sank to the bottom of the Atlantic Ocean, Ballard and his crew had discovered its final resting place. The ship lay in darkness, split in two massive pieces. Clusters of rust hung from its side, blanketing the "unsinkable" ship so many people had wanted to find.

Robert Ballard, who found *Titanic*'s final resting place, has devoted much of his life to deep-sea exploration.

5

CHAPTER 1

Hunting for Titanic

An Amazing Ship

Historians, treasure hunters, and family members of victims were lured to *Titanic* ever since it sank on April 15, 1912. They wanted to find the famous ship and discover more about its doomed **maiden** voyage.

When *Titanic* was built, people thought it was practically unsinkable. It was the largest ship of its day and had special watertight compartments. The ship was built to stay afloat even if several of these compartments filled with water. The public was stunned when the ship sank after striking an iceberg on its very first voyage.

In 1912 *Titanic* was one of the grandest ships ever built.

maiden—first

first-class passengers on
Titanic's Grand Staircase

The Washington Post.

TITANIC'S 1,470 PASSENGERS ARE NOW BEING
TRANSFERRED IN LIFEBOATS TO CUNARD LINER

People around the world anxiously awaited
more information as newspapers broke
the news that *Titanic* had sunk.

The luxury and beauty of *Titanic* was an attraction for its
passengers. The ship had large, comfortable cabins and fine dining
rooms for first-class passengers. *Titanic* carried many wealthy
passengers. Some of the people searching for *Titanic* wondered if
valuable jewelry was still onboard the ship.

FACT: More than 1,500 people lost their lives when
Titanic sank. Only 712 passengers and crew
members survived.

Chasing *Titanic*

The first ship to search for *Titanic* was *Carpathia*. Its crew rushed to the sinking ship in an effort to save lives before the ship went under.

The night *Titanic* sank, *Carpathia* heard its distress signals. It headed toward the sinking ship and picked up more than 700 survivors who were in *Titanic*'s lifeboats. *Carpathia*'s crew did not see the ship, though. *Titanic* had sunk about two hours before rescuers arrived.

Vincent Astor was one of the first to talk about locating *Titanic*. His father, John Jacob Astor, was a wealthy man who had died in the disaster.

CANADA

NORTH ATLANTIC OCEAN

UNITED STATES

where *Titanic* sank

WHERE IS IT?

For years the location of *Titanic* remained a mystery. People could not find the ship. The distress signal sent by the ship's radio operators had provided an incorrect location. The officer who calculated the ship's location was off by several miles. The depth of the ship beneath the water also kept it hidden. It was on the ocean floor more than 2 miles (3 km) beneath the surface of the ocean.

Soon after *Titanic* sank, people began to talk about finding the ship. Many interesting ideas were raised regarding how to bring it to the surface. Over the years people thought of using magnets, nylon balloons, wax, and even ping-pong balls to raise *Titanic*. But these ideas were never tried. People still were not sure where the ship rested.

In 1953 a British ship set off explosions in the area where *Titanic* sank. The people involved hoped the explosions' echoes would allow them to determine where the ship was located. But the results were of no help. *Titanic* remained hidden under the waves.

GREAT BRITAIN

IRELAND

FRANCE

SPAIN

PORTUGAL

Carpathia picked up *Titanic*'s 712 survivors and brought them to New York City.

Ballard with *Alvin* in 1986

The Right Sub for the Job

Thrusters

Even if explorers had known where *Titanic* sank, they would have had trouble reaching it. For years explorers lacked equipment that could withstand the water pressure that far below the water's surface.

Then in 1973 equipment was developed that would make it possible to find *Titanic*. That year a tiny submarine named *Alvin* was fitted with a strong **hull**. The submarine could withstand intense water pressure without being crushed. It could dive more than 2 miles (3 km) under the ocean's surface. *Alvin* was strong enough to reach *Titanic* once it was located.

HULL

Oceanographer Robert Ballard was especially interested in *Alvin*'s diving ability. Ballard loved exploring the world under the sea. He dreamed of using *Alvin* to explore *Titanic*.

thruster—a propeller on a ship that provides extra support and can move from side to side

hull—the main body of a ship or other large, heavy vehicle, including its bottoms, sides, and deck

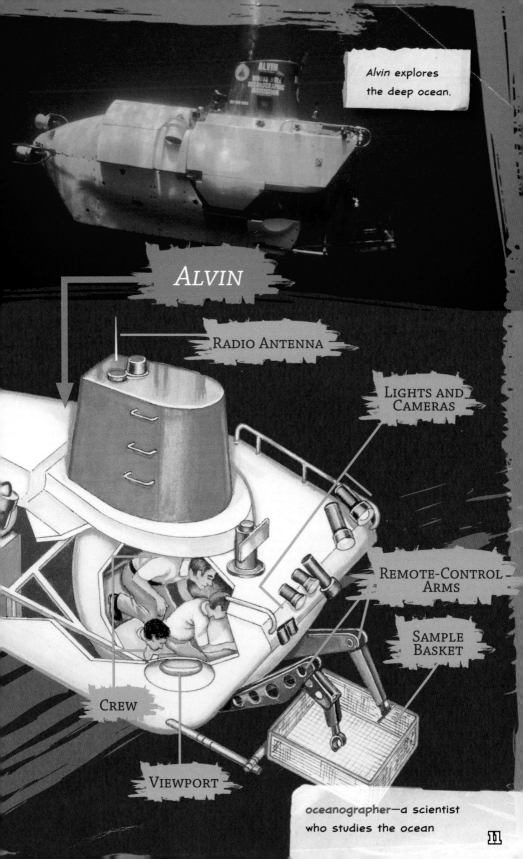

Alvin explores the deep ocean.

ALVIN

RADIO ANTENNA

LIGHTS AND CAMERAS

REMOTE-CONTROL ARMS

SAMPLE BASKET

CREW

VIEWPORT

oceanographer—a scientist who studies the ocean

Ballard's First Attempt

Before Ballard could use *Alvin* to explore *Titanic*, he had to find the ship. In 1977 he came up with a plan to use a research drill ship to try to locate *Titanic*.

Ballard and a crew sailed on *Alcoa Seaprobe* to the area near where *Titanic* had sunk. They lowered a long drill pipe through an opening in *Alcoa Seaprobe*'s hull. At the bottom of the pipe were underwater cameras and **sonar** equipment. The ship also towed a **magnetometer**. The equipment could create images of the ocean floor and locate metal objects. Ballard hoped the equipment would reveal *Titanic*'s location.

But before the equipment reached the ocean bottom, disaster struck. The drill pipe broke. It fell to the ocean floor and was never recovered.

Ballard's failure made it difficult for him to raise enough money to search for *Titanic* again. Ballard doubted he would have another chance to discover its location.

a sonar image of the sunken ship, the USS *Monitor*

An illustration shows the *Alcoa Seaprobe* taking photographs of the USS *Monitor*, a ship that sank during the Civil War (1861–1865).

sonar—a system that uses sound waves to find and create images of objects under water

Scientists prepare to launch a magnetometer in 1960.

magnetometer—a device that can tell if an object is made of metal

13

Jack Grimm's Three Strikes

After Ballard's failure, another explorer decided to try his luck in finding *Titanic*. Jack Grimm was a millionaire who loved adventure. He became Ballard's main rival in the hunt for *Titanic*.

Grimm's *Titanic* Timeline

1980

Grimm and two scientists sail to the area where *Titanic* sank. Using sonar, they find several targets that might be *Titanic*. However, bad weather and equipment troubles force them to give up the search.

1981

Grimm and his crew use another type of sonar to get a clearer look at 14 targets they think could be *Titanic*. But a magnetometer shows that none of the targets are the ship. At the end of the trip, Grimm's team lowers a video camera into the ocean. It shows a blurry object Grimm thinks is *Titanic*'s **propeller**. The scientists working with Grimm are unsure. They believe the image is too blurry to say for sure what the object is.

1983

Grimm and his crew return to the propeller site, hoping to prove the object Grimm believes to be a propeller was attached to *Titanic*. But the sonar does not show any objects large enough to be *Titanic*. High winds keep them from searching other areas. The crew returns empty handed, and Grimm's quest for *Titanic* comes to an end.

propeller—a device with rotating blades that moves a ship through the water

Jack Grimm (*left*) and his expedition team display a chart showing their 1981 *Titanic* search.

FACT: Grimm's other expeditions included searches for legendary creatures and artifacts, including the Loch Ness monster, Bigfoot, and Noah's Ark.

CHAPTER 2

Ballard Sees His Chance

Grimm's failure meant Ballard could still realize his dream of finding *Titanic*. Ballard also saw how new underwater robots, known as remotely operated underwater vehicles (ROVs), could help him overcome some of the problems with searching for the ship.

The Problems:

- *Titanic* was more than 2 miles (3 km) beneath the ocean's surface. Water pressure at that depth could crush equipment and make it dangerous for explorers.

- There is little natural light beyond 650 feet (198 meters) below sea level.

- It was costly to look for the ship, so scientists had to cover as much ground as they could in a short amount of time.

The ROV *Hercules* uses lights to show the deep ocean floor.

The Solution:

- ROVs could be operated by scientists on the surface. This was less dangerous than putting a scientist in a submarine.

- ROVs could stay underwater for days and withstand high water pressure.

- The ROVs carried lights that made underwater objects visible and used special cameras to take pictures.

- Robotic arms could set up scientific equipment and collect samples. However, Ballard did not plan on removing any objects from the Titanic wreck, so he would use a robotic arm to carry a camera.

- The ROVs could send a video feed to the surface right away, helping searchers cover a larger area in less time. If they didn't see anything of importance, they could move on to a different area.

A robotic arm collects a sample of coral.

Argo

Strobe lights

Lamp

Sidescan sonar

15 feet (4.6 m) long

Weight: 4,000 pounds (1,800 kilograms)

Argo

In 1983 Ballard worked with a team at the Woods Hole Oceanographic Institution in Massachusetts. Together they developed a new ROV called *Argo*.

Scientists could lower *Argo* more than 1 mile (2 km) under the ocean's surface. They used a long cable to attach *Argo* to a ship and tow it 50 to 100 feet (15 to 30 m) above the bottom of the ocean. The ROV acted as underwater eyes for scientists on the surface. Its video cameras sent live images through a cable. One camera could zoom in on objects for a closer look.

Argo's lights made objects visible in the darkness of the deep ocean. In addition, its cameras made light seem 10,000 times brighter. *Argo* also had side and front sonars to create images of a large area.

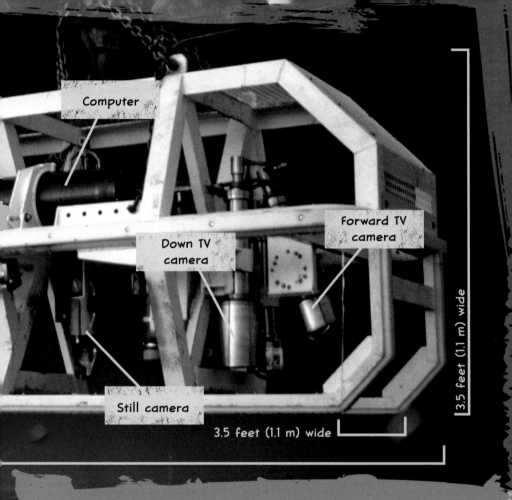

Computer

Forward TV camera

Down TV camera

Still camera

3.5 feet (1.1 m) wide

3.5 feet (1.1 m) wide

FACT: *Argo* got its name from a ship in the Greek myth Jason and the Golden Fleece. In the myth the Greek hero Jason sails on *Argo* while he looks for the Golden Fleece.

Argo hunts for *Titanic* in 1985.

Jason Jr.

Once researchers found *Titanic*, *Argo* would be too large to get inside the sunken ship. Scientists needed a smaller robot for this job. Ballard worked with the Woods Hole Oceanographic Institution to create the perfect robot for this task.

Jason Jr.'s small size made it ideal for exploring the tight spaces of shipwrecks.

What Jason Jr. Was

The robot *Jason Jr.* was also called *JJ*. *JJ* was perfectly suited to fit inside *Titanic*. *JJ* looked a bit like a lawnmower with no handle. It had lights, cameras, and motors. It was small enough to be carried on the front of the submarine *Alvin*.

How JJ Worked

Scientists used a cable to attach *JJ* to *Alvin*. A pilot inside the submarine sent signals through the cable to control *JJ*. Thrusters propelled the small robot forward, up, and to the side. Using these movements, *JJ* could swim inside *Titanic*.

What JJ Did

Once inside *Titanic*, *JJ* could take pictures with its video camera and still camera. The images were recorded so others could see them as well.

JJ explores *Titanic*'s hull in 1986.

NAME	ALVIN	ANGUS
DECADE BUILT	1960s	1970s
PEOPLE COULD RIDE IN IT	Yes	No
CONTROLLED WITH A CABLE	No	Yes
TOWED BY A SHIP	No	Yes
COULD FIT INTO SMALL SPACES	No	No
PROPELLED BY THRUSTERS	Yes	No
MAXIMUM DIVING DEPTH	14,800 feet (4,500 m)	20,000 feet (6,100 m)

Old and Reliable

Not all of the equipment Ballard would use on the *Titanic* search mission was new. He saw that an older piece of equipment called *ANGUS* could also be useful.

Scientists built *ANGUS* in the 1970s. They called it a sled because it carried three cameras in a 12-foot (4-m) frame. *ANGUS* could hang from a ship by a thick wire. Its cameras pointed downward and together they could take photos of an area 200 feet (60 m) wide.

ANGUS was built to work in rough seas. Its steel frame kept its cameras from being damaged if the sled hit a rock. The tough piece of equipment would be especially useful if seas were too rough for the ROVs.

ARGO	JASON JR.
1980s	1980s
No	No
Yes	Yes
Yes	No
No	Yes
No	Yes
20,000 feet (6,100 m)	21,400 feet (6,500 m)

ANGUS hung in the water on a thick wire and was towed by a ship.

Ballard (*center*) reviews charts with crew members aboard *Knorr*.

Titanic Team

Ballard needed more than the latest equipment to help him find *Titanic*. He also needed people with many different skills to make the mission a success. Some crew members would operate the ROVs, cameras, and other equipment needed to find *Titanic*. Other crew members would focus on sailing the ship.

Crew members needed to know how to keep the ship on its proper path. This ship the team members would be sailing on, *Knorr*, had to move slowly and precisely in order to make sure the images sent by the underwater cameras were as clear as possible.

The Search Squad

Ballard's team was split into three different groups called watches. Each watch would work four hours in the morning and four at night:

FLYERS
Earl Young, Martin Bowen, and Emile Bergeron controlled a cable attached to *Argo*. The robot took pictures of the bottom of the ocean.

NAVIGATORS
Steve Gegg, Tom Crook, and Cathy Offinger tracked the location of the *Knorr* and *Argo*.

DRIVERS
Watch leaders Jean-Louis Michel, Jean Jarry, and Bernard Pillaud steered *Knorr* and controlled its speed.

ENGINEERS
Stu Harris, Tom Dettweiler, and Bob Squires fixed problems with *Argo*.

SONAR OPERATORS
George Rey, Terry Snyder, and Jim Saint identified images on *Argo*'s sonar screen.

DOCUMENTATION TEAM
Bill Lange, Emory Kristof, and Ralph White logged the details of the search.

DATA LOGGERS
Sharon Callahan, Georgina Baker, and Lisa Schwartz mapped the search area.

Other Crew Members

CAPTAIN
Richard Bowen supervised the ship's operations and crew.

ROBOTIC RESEARCHER
Dana Yoerger worked on tracking software for *Argo*.

Ballard acted as the chief scientist, overseeing the mission.

International Assistance

Ballard knew it would take time to do a thorough search for *Titanic*. However, he and his crew would only have time to spend a few weeks in the area where the ship sank. Ballard thought it would most likely take more than a few weeks to find the ship. He needed help. He flew to Paris, France, and asked a group of French scientists to assist with his search.

Ballard had worked with French researcher Jean-Louis Michel in the past. In the 1970s they had studied a ridge under the Atlantic Ocean together. Now Michel and scientists from the French Research Institute for Exploitation of the Sea were happy to help Ballard search for *Titanic*. The French scientists wanted to test their new sonar technology. The fame and mystery surrounding *Titanic* also lured them.

The French crew had a new sonar scanner to search the ocean floor. This tool would help them find targets that could be *Titanic*. Ballard's team would visit later and send down a robot to take a closer look at any targets of interest. Working together French and American teams could conduct a better search than if each group worked alone.

The French team prepares to launch its sonar equipment from its research ship, *Le Suroit*.

CHAPTER 3

Discovery!

Mapping a Search Area

Now that he had the right equipment and team for the *Titanic* search, Ballard had to zero in on a search area. When deciding where to look, Ballard and the leaders of the French team considered the location given by *Titanic*'s crew the night the ship sank. They read information about ice provided by other ships in the area that night.

The team also looked at the place *Carpathia* had found the lifeboats and how the ocean's **current** could have carried them away from the ship. They determined the ship was east of the position reported by its crew. The team mapped a main search area covering 115 square miles (298 square km).

As *Titanic* sank, its radio operators frantically sent out distress signals, which were picked up by *Carpathia*'s operator (*right*). However, the coordinates *Titanic*'s crew provided were incorrect. Luckily *Carpathia* found the survivors anyway.

FACT: Ballard's search area was almost twice the size of Washington, D.C.

WHAT COULD GO WRONG?

Although he had a solid search plan and the latest equipment, Ballard knew it was possible his team might not locate *Titanic*. Potential problems included:

- **Mud:** The ship might be hidden beneath an underwater mudslide that had occurred during an earthquake in 1929.
- **Canyons:** The ship may have fallen into a deep underwater canyon.
- **Breakage:** *Titanic* may have broken apart into small pieces.
- **Shadows:** The ship might be behind an underwater ridge, preventing it from being viewed with sonar.
- **Weather:** High waves could make it difficult for the sonar to work properly.
- **Time:** The team's equipment was needed for other projects. The group had only about five weeks to use it.

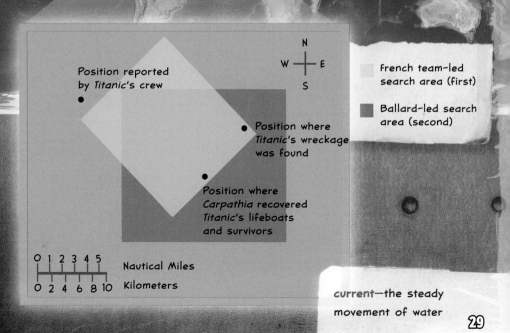

Position reported by *Titanic*'s crew

Position where *Titanic*'s wreckage was found

Position where *Carpathia* recovered *Titanic*'s lifeboats and survivors

N
W — E
S

French team-led search area (first)

Ballard-led search area (second)

0 1 2 3 4 5 Nautical Miles

0 2 4 6 8 10 Kilometers

current—the steady movement of water

29

Scanning Struggles

The French team's *Titanic* search began on July 5, 1985. They lowered their sonar into the water and began traveling in a pattern that looked like they were mowing the lawn over the ocean bottom.

For approximately four weeks, the French crew scanned the bottom of the ocean. Bad weather kept them from covering as much ground as they wanted to. They did not find *Titanic*. However, their work allowed Ballard to rule out most of this area when he began his part of the search.

THE FRENCH SONAR SEARCH

1. The French sonar system used an object that looked like a big red torpedo. They called it *poisson*, which is French for "fish." It hung on a cable and was towed by the ship.

2. The "fish" sent out sound waves that swept across the bottom of the ocean.

3. When the unit's sound waves bounced back to the ship, the signals created computer images called shadow graphs. These shadow graphs were almost as clear as black-and-white photos.

4. A magnetometer trailed behind the "fish." It helped the crew determine if an object was made of metal or if it was a large underwater rock formation.

 **FACT:** The cable towing the sonar was 2.5 miles (4 km) long. This is the same length as 220 semitrucks with trailers end to end.

The French team prepares for a night launch of its sonar.

A ceramic bowl and other *Titanic* debris lie scattered on the ocean floor near where the ship went down.

Zeroing in on Debris

After the French team failed to find *Titanic*, it was Ballard's turn to search for the ship. Many people believed *Titanic* sank in one piece. But Ballard thought the ship split into two parts as it sank. A survivor who was near the ship when it went down described how it broke apart. Ballard thought this description was correct. Rather than look for the ship itself, he would look for its debris. It was likely that a long trail of items spilled out of the ship as it sank. Finding this trail would lead Ballard to *Titanic*. The debris that fell from *Titanic* would cover a large area. Ballard thought it would be easier to find the debris field than the ship itself.

SECRET MISSIONS

Ballard was very hopeful the debris would lead him to *Titanic*. He had used this same tactic to study wreckage from two sunken submarines in the early 1980s. These missions for the U.S. Navy were kept secret. Ballard could not talk about them until years later. On these missions Ballard noticed items from the submarines did not sink in a single clump. Heavier objects sank first. Lighter ones drifted on the current before falling to the bottom of the ocean. This trail of debris formed a pattern that led Ballard to the main wreckage of the submarines.

" By following the crumbs, we would find *Titanic*. "

—Robert Ballard

debris from *Titanic*

Ballard (*standing*) and other members of the team study monitors showing images of the ocean floor.

Trouble and Tension

Ballard and his crew began their search in an area about 350 miles (563 km) off the coast of Newfoundland, Canada, on August 25, 1985. *Argo*'s cameras captured images of the sea floor. All day and night crew members took turns watching the monitors, looking for man-made objects. *Argo* gave them a good view of the ocean bottom, but all they saw was mud and sand.

KNORR

As the days dragged on, crew members became
discouraged. They did not see any objects that told them they
were near *Titanic*. They began to lose hope as they neared the
edge of their search area.

By August 31 even Ballard was
worried. A storm was on its way that
would rock the ship and make it difficult
to hold *Argo* steady. The crew had only
five days before they had to return to
port in Massachusetts. Ballard feared
the mission would end in failure.

*Knorr was built to help scientists
study the world's oceans.*

Titanic Sighting

Ballard went to his cabin shortly after midnight on September 1, 1985. He was tired and discouraged. Then the cook stopped by and told him the crew wanted to see him.

Ballard hurried to the control room. The crew replayed the tape of what they had just seen on the monitors. Ballard watched as pieces of wreckage appeared on the screen and then a boiler, which the crew had identified as one from *Titanic*. Then *Titanic*'s portholes and a piece of railing came into view. Ballard was so excited, he could barely speak. Then the entire room erupted in joyful celebration.

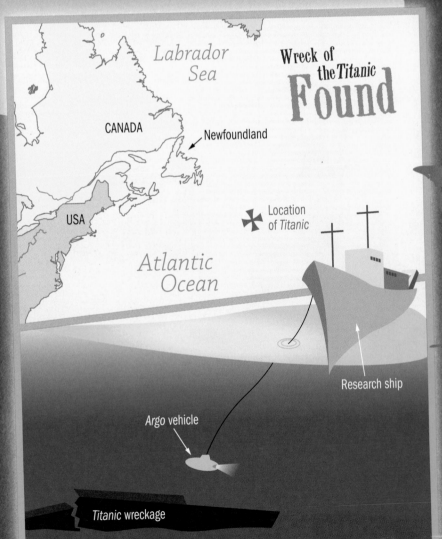

Labrador Sea

Wreck of the Titanic
Found

CANADA

Newfoundland

USA

Location of *Titanic*

Atlantic Ocean

Research ship

Argo vehicle

Titanic wreckage

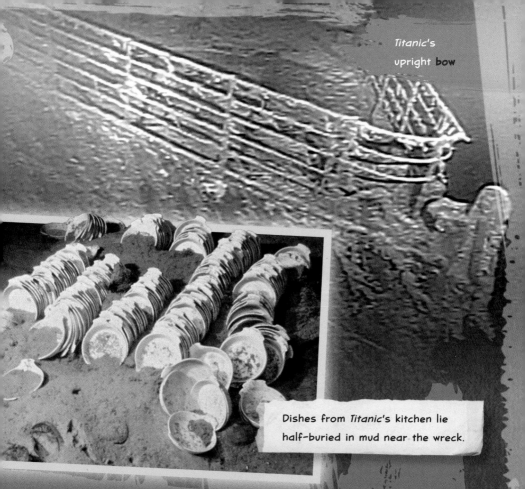

Titanic's upright **bow**

Dishes from *Titanic's* kitchen lie half-buried in mud near the wreck.

Over the next few days, *Argo* and *ANGUS* took video and photos of *Titanic's* wreck. Ballard learned several things:

★ *Titanic* was upright.

★ The crow's nest was lying on the deck.

★ Coal, dishes, and bottles were in the debris field.

★ The **stern** was lying apart from the rest of the ship.

Ballard wanted to learn more about the ship's remains, but he was out of time for his mission. The equipment and crew were needed for other projects, and they had to return to port. Ballard's *Titanic* mission would have to be continued.

bow—the front of a ship
stern—the rear of a ship

CHAPTER 4
Exploring
Titanic

A Closer Look

Ballard was not done exploring *Titanic*. In July 1986 he began another mission to learn more about the sunken luxury liner. This time *Alvin* and *JJ* gave him a firsthand look.

RUSTICLES

Among the odd sights Ballard saw on his trip to *Titanic* were rusticles that hung from the ship's bow. Rusticles look like red-brown icicles. They are created by bacteria and fungi that live off rusting metal. *Titanic's* rusticles crumbled when *Alvin* passed them.

Rusticles hang off the side of *Titanic*.

JJ's Journey

After a 2.5-hour descent, *Alvin*'s pilot set the submarine on the ship's deck. Now it was time for *JJ* to go to work. While attached to *Alvin* with a cable, *JJ* made its way in through an opening in *Titanic*'s deck. The robot traveled down the Grand Staircase and took video images. Ballard saw the beautiful wood that had once been inside the ship was gone. Tiny creatures known as wood-boring mollusks had eaten it. However, a pillar and fancy light fixtures remained.

Ballard spent almost two weeks using *Alvin* and *JJ* to gather video of the sunken ship. He saw the remains of the captain's cabin. In the debris field near the ship, he saw plates, sinks, bathtubs, doorknobs, windows, and a safe. On one of his last dives in *Alvin* Ballard left a plaque on the ship's stern. It honored the victims of the disaster. He hoped others would allow the ship to rest as a memorial to those who died.

RMS Titanic, Inc., brought a piece of Titanic's hull to the surface in 1998.

Undersea Attraction

Ballard hoped people would leave *Titanic* undisturbed. Others, however, were drawn to the site to take photos, study the ship, and gather artifacts.

A company called RMS Titanic, Inc., visited *Titanic* in 1987. The group recovered a bell, a compass, dishes, a porthole, and more than 1,000 other items from the ship's debris field. Its explorers later returned to the site to gather items for museum displays. In the first 25 years after *Titanic*'s discovery, RMS Titanic, Inc., recovered more than 5,500 items from the area around the ship. Some of the items recovered from the ship's debris field were ordinary, such as keys and dishes. Others were valuable objects, including jewelry that had belonged to wealthy passengers.

Recovered from *Titanic*

a third-class passenger's vest, which was found in a suitcase

a statue from the ship's Grand Staircase

a hat worn by one of *Titanic*'s bakers

a bracelet with the name "Amy" written in diamonds

Solving *Titanic's* Mysteries

Studying *Titanic*'s wreckage has helped researchers understand how the ship may have sunk:

1 The watertight compartments in *Titanic*'s bow filled with water after it struck an iceberg.

2 The bow sank.

3 The stern of the ship rose into the air.

4 The weight of the water in the bow caused the ship to snap in two.

5 The bow shot toward the bottom and landed nose first.

6 The stern flooded and sank.

7 Debris spilled out of the stern, its decks collapsed, and it landed in a gigantic, mangled mess on the ocean floor.

The Fate of *Titanic*

Controversy swirls over how to treat *Titanic*'s remains. Some fear visitors will damage the ship. Others want to carefully visit the ship to study it. Artifacts from *Titanic* are very valuable. They are also very fragile. Without careful preservation, they can decay. When RMS Titanic, Inc., brings artifacts to the surface, it preserves and records each object. The most fragile objects are kept in storage, where they can be protected from further decay. Many objects are sturdy enough for travel. These artifacts are exhibited in museums around the world, where they are seen by millions. *Titanic* may rest in darkness miles under the ocean, but it continues to fascinate people around the world.

Artifacts recovered from *Titanic* are displayed at an exhibit in Paris, France.

What to Do?

Since *Titanic*'s discovery, many people have weighed in on whether or not people should explore the wreck further.

Visit It

"MOST OF THE PEOPLE GOING OUT THERE WITH US HAVE AN ABSOLUTE REVERENCE FOR *TITANIC*."

—Rob McCallum, Deep Ocean Expeditions, a diving company

"IF WE DON'T BRING THEM UP, YEARS FROM NOW, STUDENTS WILL ASK 'WHY? WHY WHEN YOU HAD THE TECHNOLOGY, WHY DIDN'T YOU DO IT?'"

—Robert DiSogra, cofounder of Titanic International Society, a historical group

Preserve It

"TO US IT'S A GRAVE SITE – WHY DISTURB IT ANY FURTHER?"

— Edward Kamuda, president of the Titanic Historical Society

"TAKING ITEMS FROM *TITANIC* IS 'GRAVE ROBBING.'"

—Eva Hart, *Titanic* survivor

Eva Hart

Glossary

boiler (BOY-ler)—a device that creates steam to power a ship's engine

bow (BAU)—the front of a ship

current (KUHR-uhnt)—the steady movement of water

hull (HUL)—the main body of a ship or other large, heavy vehicle, including its bottoms, sides, and deck

magnetometer (mag–ne-TOM-i-tuhr)—a device that can tell if an object is made of metal

maiden (MAY-duhn)—first

oceanographer (oh-shuh-NOG-ruh-fur)—a scientist who studies the ocean

propeller (pruh-PEL-ur)—a device with rotating blades that moves a ship through the water

sonar (SOH-nar)—a system that uses sound waves to find and create images of underwater objects

stern (STURN)—the rear of a ship

thruster (THRUHST-ur)—a propeller on a ship that provides extra support and can move from side to side

Read More

Driscoll, Laura. *Titanic: The Story Lives On!* New York: Penguin Young Readers, 2012.

Price, Sean Stewart. *The Kids' Guide to Titanic*. Kids' Guides. North Mankato, Minn.: Capstone Press, 2012.

Stewart, David. *You Wouldn't Want to Sail on the Titanic!: One Voyage You'd Rather Not Make.* You Wouldn't Want to … New York: Franklin Watts, An Imprint of Scholastic Inc., 2013.

Critical Thinking Using the Common Core

1. What challenges did Robert Ballard face as he searched for *Titanic*? How did he overcome them? (Key Ideas and Details)

2. Look at the chart on pages 22 and 23 that explains some of the different tools Ballard used to find *Titanic*. Using this chart and online resources, explain how underwater research vehicles and equipment have changed over time. How did these tools help Ballard find *Titanic*? (Integration of Knowledge and Ideas)

3. Many people, including Ballard, believe future explorers should leave the *Titanic* wreck alone. Come up with a few reasons why people might agree with this belief. Do you think *Titanic* should be explored further? Why or why not? (Integration of Knowledge and Ideas)

Internet Sites

FactHound offers a safe, fun way to find Internet sites related to this book. All of the sites on FactHound have been researched by our staff.

Here's all you do:

Visit *www.facthound.com*

Type in this code: 9781491404188

Index